EYEWITNESS
EXPLORERS

Insects

Written by
STEVE PARKER

DK

DORLING KINDERSLEY
London · New York · Stuttgart

A DORLING KINDERSLEY BOOK

Senior editor Susan McKeever
Art editor Thomas Keenes
Editor Jodi Block
Senior art editor Jacquie Gulliver
Production Catherine Semark
Photography by Frank Greenaway
Editorial consultant John Feltwell

This Eyewitness ® Explorers book
first published in Great Britain in 1992 by
Dorling Kindersley Limited
9 Henrietta Street
Covent Garden
London WC2E 8PS

Reprinted 1997

A CIP catalogue for this book is available from the British Library.

ISBN 07513 6095 3

Colour reproduction by Colourscan, Singapore
Printed in Spain by Artes Gráficas Toledo, S.A.
D.L.TO: 630 1997
Visit us on the World Wide Web at
http://www.dk.com

Contents

Looking at insects

Many insects are so small that you cannot see them in detail, so they might not seem interesting. But with a few bits of equipment and some practice, you can soon learn about their fascinating ways and habits. Look for insects on leaves and flowers, under stones and logs, and in the soil.

Pencil-written notes won't run if it rains.

Magnifier
A magnifying lens shows an insect in amazing detail. Place it over the insect so it can't run away. But don't keep it trapped for too long!

Use a notepad with a stiff back.

Drawing
Make a sketch of what you see. Label features such as wings or unusually-shaped legs. Note the insect's size, colour, and where it lives. You can finish the sketch later – and you'll soon improve with practice.

The common tiger beetle, with its bright green colour, is easy to spot running along the sand on sunny days.

Make a pooter

A pooter picks up small or fast-moving insects safely. You'll need thin clear plastic, modelling clay, two wide plastic drinking straws, sticky tape, and a bit of muslin.

Straw *Modelling clay*

This bit goes inside the tube.

1 Roll the plastic into a tube 3-4 cm across and sticky-tape it. Tape the muslin over the end of one straw.

2 Make blobs of clay for each end of the tube. Fix a straw in each blob, with the muslin inside the tube.

The muslin stops the insect from going into your mouth.

3 Suck the muslin-ended straw. Air rushes in through the other straw, carrying small items with it. Loosen the clay blob to remove things from the tube.

4 Hold the pooter near an insect on a leaf or a flower and suck.

Move and lift small insects on a paintbrush, to avoid squashing them.

Storage jar

A clean glass jar with air-holes in the lid makes a good insect home. Always put the insects back as soon as you can.

9

What is an insect?

There are more kinds of insects than any other kind of animal. There are gnats and midges almost too small to see, irritating flies, stinging wasps, and huge beetles. Check that a creature is an insect by the 3 + 3 rule. A typical insect has three parts to its body and three pairs of legs.

A butterfly has four large, colourful wings.

Ladybird
This small, tough creature is a kind of insect called a beetle. Under its hard body covering are two wings, ready to fly away if the ladybird meets trouble.

Butterfly
The butterfly is a fairly large and delicate insect. Like many other insects, it has two antennae or "feelers" on its head. These can smell, as well as feel.

Centipede

Not insects
Count the legs on these animals. Eight legs usually means a spider, and 14 a woodlouse. Lots of legs means a centipede, even more is a millipede. Only insects have six legs.

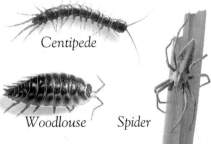

Woodlouse   *Spider*

Insect in close-up

The common wasp shows all the main parts of an insect. It has four wings, although many insects only have two. The front and back wings on each side are linked together by hooks, so they flap as one. Wasps have bright yellow and black markings to warn other animals that they are not good to eat. Wasps have a powerful sting, so try not to annoy them!

Feelers

An insect's head has two big eyes, feelers, and mouthparts for biting.

The legs have tiny claws at the end for hanging on to plants.

An insect's leg has joints which bend as it walks and runs.

Wasps have a very small "waist" separating their thorax and abdomen.

The middle part, the thorax, has wings and legs on the outside, and large muscles inside.

Tubes called veins stiffen the see-through wings.

The end part, the abdomen, contains the guts for digesting food, and the reproductive parts for breeding.

11

Legs and leaping

Most adult insects move swiftly on their six legs. They may not seem very fast to us, because they are so small. But if an ant was as big as a human, it could run five times faster than an Olympic sprinter. And a human-sized flea could leap over a 40-storey building.

Leg joints

Like all insects, this bush cricket has six jointed legs, each with four main parts. It also has special "ears" on its front legs for hearing sounds made by other bush crickets.

Before it leaps, this speckled bush cricket makes sure its feet have a good, firm grip on the branch.

The cricket's "ear" lies just below the knee joint.

The cricket looks around to make sure it is safe to jump.

Look before you leap

Insects with very long legs, such as crickets, grasshoppers, and fleas, are usually good leapers. The cricket folds its long legs back on each other when it gets ready to leap.

The cricket opens its speckled wings, ready to flutter a short distance, and then glide to land in a safe place.

Into the air
Powerful muscles in the legs straighten the "hip" joints and the "knee" joints, so that the whole leg is straight. The parts of the leg work like long levers, to fling the cricket into the air. Your arm straightens in the same way when you throw a ball.

The cricket can kick out with its spiny legs, to defend itself.

Hip joint

Knee joint

Spine

Expert digger
The mole cricket's back legs are powerful for pushing through soil. It also has short, wide front legs. These work like shovels to help it dig tunnels in the soil.

Singing insects
A grasshopper chirps by rubbing its back leg along a stiff vein in the front wing. The leg has small teeth on it, like a comb, which buzz and vibrate. It sings to attract mates and warn rivals.

13

Walking on water

Where air and water meet, a stretchy "skin" forms at the water's surface. Because many insects are tiny, this skin is strong enough to support them. Some bugs and beetles can run on it. Underwater insects hang from it and poke their breathing tubes up into the air, or collect air bubbles.

Rear legs are rudders for steering. Middle legs push the skater across the surface. Front legs detect ripples from struggling prey.

Water boatman
Look out for the water boatman swimming just under the surface of rivers, lakes, and ponds. It rows along on its back, with its large rear legs. It hunts tiny fish, tadpoles, and insects. Don't touch – it can give a painful nip!

Surface skater
The pondskater, a kind of water bug, skims over the water surface. Waterproof hairs on its feet make dimples in the water, as it chases insects trapped in the surface skin.

Whirligigs
These small, black beetles swim in groups, spinning on the water surface. They eat dead creatures that fall into the pond.

The whirligig beetle has two pairs of eyes, for seeing above and below the surface.

Make an insect aquarium

Study insects from ponds or streams in a small aquarium for a week or two. Use a net to catch them, and put them back afterwards. Which insects live near the surface or on the bottom? When are they most active?

Many pond insects can fly. Keep a lid with a close-weave net or mesh on the tank.

Moulting insects such as mayflies need plants or sticks above the surface, to crawl up.

Pondweed is food, and insects cling to it and hide in it.

Bottom-dwellers such as caddisfly larvae like to hide under stones.

1 A glass fish tank makes a good insect aquarium, but any large bowl will do. Put gravel and small stones on the bottom. Add pond or fresh water, and plants to make the tank about half-full. Let it settle for a few days, then add your insects.

Change two jamjars full of tank water for pond water each day to keep the water fresh and provide food.

2 Keep the tank in a well-lit but cool corner of the room. The water will get too hot in bright sunlight.

3 Tiny plants called algae may grow as a green "scum" on the sides of the tank. Rub them off with a sponge tied to a stick, and filter them out of the water with a tea-strainer.

On the wing

Most insects have wings and can fly at some stage in their lives. Insect wings are thin and light, and are stiffened by a network of tubes called veins. Strong muscles in the middle section of the insect provide the power for flapping.

Lacy wings
The lacewing's beautiful pattern of veins in its four wings looks like finely woven lace. This insect flies mainly at night.

Beetle take-off
Beetles have four wings. But the front pair are hard and tough. They cover the beetle's back and protect the long, folded, flying wings underneath. This cardinal beetle is preparing for take-off.

The cardinal beetle lifts its red protective wing covers.

It unfolds and spreads out its main pair of flying wings.

Up and away

The long see-through wings, with their strengthening veins, move so fast that they become a blur. The beetle flies off to look for more food.

Main wings do all the flapping.

The hard wing-cases do not flap at all. The beetle holds them clear of the main flying wings.

Speeding up

With each beat, the main wings push air downwards. This lifts the cardinal beetle upwards. Then the wings also begin to push air backward, so that the beetle moves forward.

The beetle beats its wings faster and faster until they reach flying speed. Pushing with its legs against the flower, it springs away. In a flash, the beetle is airborne.

The beetle straightens its legs and holds them down, away from the fast-moving wings.

Expert flier

Hoverflies are expert fliers. They can hover above flowers, then dart off and reappear a short distance away. They can move in any direction – including backwards.

Feeding time

Some insects can eat almost anything. Cockroaches have strong chewing mouthparts to eat stale food, dirt, even paper and leather. Other insects have specially shaped mouths. Bugs have a hollow, needle-shaped beak, to pierce and suck sap from plants. Look at plant leaves for evidence of hungry insects.

Nipping weevil

Weevils are kinds of beetles. They have a long curved "snout" called a rostrum, with tiny jaws at the end. They bite small pieces of leaves and other plant parts. If you look on a nettle plant you may spot a weevil.

The curved "fang" is called a mandible.

Spearing prey

This diving beetle larva has large pointed "fangs" for spearing prey. It squirts special juices into the tadpole that dissolve its body into soup. The beetle larva then sucks up the mushy meal.

The long, tube-shaped mouth is called a proboscis.

This is a hummingbird hawk-moth – it feeds like a hummingbird.

Built-in straw

Butterflies and moths have mouths shaped like drinking straws. When they are not feeding the straw is coiled up. To suck sweet nectar from flowers, it is uncoiled into a straight tube.

Ant attack

Ants have strong jaws, called mandibles, which can bite and cut up food and enemies. This bulldog ant has especially big mandibles. They seize and chop up other insects for food. Don't touch – bulldog ants can bite!

The ant's mouth is just underneath the base of the mandibles.

Each mandible moves at a hinge joint where it joins the head

Spikes along the inner edge of the mandibles give it extra grip.

Munching lice

Bark lice live under loose bark on trees, biting and chewing the small moulds which grow there. Some nibble on books, especially damp ones. So keep your books in a dry place!

Insect-eye view

What does an insect see? Probably a very different view of the world to us. Most insects have eyes, made of many separate sections, called ommatidia (say *om-a-tid-ee-a*). Each section sees a small part of the surroundings. The whole view may look like a patchwork.

Simple eyes

Besides two main eyes (compound eyes), many insects also have several smaller eyes. These are known as simple eyes or ocelli (say *o-sell-ee*), and they do not have separate sections. They probably just detect blurs of light or dark.

A cicada has three simple eyes.

The dragonfly's huge compound eyes take up most of its head.

The dragonfly can see in front, below, and behind, all at the same time.

All-round vision

It's not easy to get close to a dragonfly, because it can see all around it at the same time. Imagine being able to see behind yourself without turning your neck! Dragonflies hunt by sight.

Each ommatidium has a transparent top to let in light.

Light is refracted, or broken-up, into rainbow patterns off the tiny ommatidia.

What big eyes . . .

Dragonflies have the biggest eyes of any insect. This is a front view of the common darter dragonfly shown opposite. Each eye has up to 5,000 ommatidia! Many insects can tell colours apart, and many, such as moths, can see clearly at night.

The eyes look for danger, mates, rivals, and egg-laying places.

Seeing the invisible

Many insects can detect ultra-violet light. This is light from the Sun that we cannot see (but it gives us a tan). Guide lines on petals only show up in ultra-violet light. Honey bees see them and follow them to the nectar.

Touch and feeling

A good sense of touch helps insects to detect air movements when flying, and to cling onto leaves and stems. Insects feel for footholds when crawling, for food when feeding, and for holes and cracks when hiding.

Antennae detect scents, tastes, and currents of air.

Just sitting on a leaf, the chafer beetle keeps its antennae closed

Branching out

Insect antennae are very sensitive to touch. The chafer beetle has branched, fan-shaped antennae. Normally it keeps them closed. When it takes off, the beetle fans out the antennae. This makes it more sensitive to wind currents and any smells in the air.

When in flight, it fans its antennae out.

Extra long antennae

The long-horned moth's thin antennae are over twice as long as its body. They bend and wave using even thinner muscles inside them. Big groups of moths dance around trees on sunny days. Their antennae stop them from bumping into each other.

The antenna is sensitive to air movements, smells, and vibrations.

Long horns
It's no mystery how longhorn beetles got their name. Most of them have very, very long antennae. They live in forests around the world. This one is called the victory longhorn.

Each antenna is made up of about ten segments.

Antenna is attached to the head by a flexible joint so that the beetle can move it about.

Cave dweller
The cave cricket needs long antennae, for it lives in dark caves. The cricket feels its way by "tap-tapping" with its antennae, in the same way that you would tap with a stick to find your way about, with your eyes closed.

Hairs on the legs pick up vibrations.

The beetle's wings are folded under hard, protective cases.

Taste and smell

Insects do not have a nose for smelling and a tongue for tasting, like we do. Instead, they have tiny taste buds on many parts of the body, mainly on their mouthparts and antennae, and also on their feet! The main parts for detecting smells floating in the air are the antennae.

The bluebottle is a common sight in kitchens.

Fussy flies
Tasting and smelling usually help an insect to find either food or a mate. This bluebottle fly smells the syrup, which could be food. It lands and checks by tasting, to see if it is good to eat.

The fly spreads digestive juices on the food, which is like vomiting over it!

Fly has taste buds on its feet. These are the first parts to touch the food.

Fly dabs up dissolved food with its sponge-like mouthparts.

insects.
nd,
it and
apping
nts or
r!

Follow the smell
When a searching ant finds plentiful food, it lays a trail of invisible scent on the ground, leading back to the nest. The other ants follow the trail and so find the food easily.

ned chamber
builds a special
he produces a
floats into the
ale bark beetle
help but follow
ell trail to him.

ts are attracted to each
taste it, do they stay or fly
ure water? Can you?

e
must be
comes
female
hungry,

nny summer
e dishes
a table, 60-
art. Note
ects visit
ur notebook.

3 Butterflies and wasps smell the sweet syrup, which they eat as food. Flies smell the meat and come to lay eggs, since their maggots eat flesh.

25

The mating game

Most insects need to mate in order to make mor
The female must mate with a male of her own ki
before she can lay eggs. Usually the male seeks o
courts the female. Courtship involves dancing,
the body, releasing a smell, and even flashing lig
fighting your partn

*The glow comes from
the underside of the
female's body.*

Lighting up time
The glowworm is not a worm;
it's a type of beetle. At night the
female makes a yellowish light.
This attracts a male glowworm
who mates with her.

Perfu
The male bark beetle
mating chamber, the
tempting smell tha
air. When the fer
detects it, she can't
the sn

*Male mantis has had
its head eaten off.*

Meal for a ma
The male mant
very careful as h
near to the larg
to mate. If she i
she may eat him

Mating bugs

These shieldbugs are mating. The male passes his sperm from an opening in his rear end, into the female's opening. The sperm join up with the eggs in the female's body. When she lays the eggs, they are ready to develop into young shieldbugs.

Both partners keep still while mating, so they are at less risk from predators.

The sperm pass from the male shieldbug to the female.

If you see insects joined together like this on a leaf or a twig, leave them alone.

The green shieldbug has a very strong covering that protects its body, like a warrior's shield.

The shieldbugs hold on tight to the twig.

27

Laying eggs

Each kind of insect finds the best place to lay its eggs. In the wrong place, the eggs could dry out, get too wet, go mouldy, or be eaten. Also, the young insects need food nearby when they hatch. A dungfly lays eggs in fresh droppings, because this is what the maggots eat when they hatch!

The female checks the plant is the right one before she lays.

Life underneath a leaf

The underside of a groundsel or ragwort leaf is the ideal place to look for the shiny yellow eggs of a cinnabar moth. The females lay eggs there because the caterpillars (developing moths) eat the same leaves when they hatch. This is called laying eggs on the food plant.

She lays about 30 eggs on the leaf's underside, hidden from most egg-eaters.

The wood wasp taps and prods the wood with her ovipositor, feeling for the best place to drill.

Drilling deep

All female insects lay their eggs through a tube called the ovipositor. In some insects, such as this ichneumon (*ik-new-men*) wasp, the ovipositor is like a long needle. It drills deep under the wood's surface, and the eggs slip out of its tip.

Underwater eggs

Insects such as damselflies and dragonflies lay their eggs in or near water, because the young live in water after hatching. The female damselfly pushes her thin abdomen under the surface and glues her eggs to the plant stems below.

The male damselfly holds onto the female while she lays her eggs underwater.

The damselfly needs to push really hard to get her body through the water's surface "skin".

Eggs in a purse

To protect her eggs from danger, the cockroach lays them into a bag or purse, called an ootheca. She produces this smooth, tough purse from her abdomen.

The leathery bag contains two rows of eggs.

Home sweet home

The female cockroach carries the purse around for a few days. Then she tucks it into a safe home, such as a warm corner or crack, and glues it firmly in position. The young develop and hatch two months later, as worm-like larvae.

Changing shape

The worm-like stage of the beetle's life is called a larva.

Many newly hatched insects look nothing like the adults they will become. Young flies, beetles, butterflies, bees, ants, and wasps all look a bit like worms. They grow bigger, then change their body shape completely, and turn into adults. This way of growing up is called complete metamorphosis.

As the larva grows, it must split its skin and wriggle out.

New, bigger skin forms underneath. Changing skins like this is called moulting.

The larva
A newly hatched larva of a flour beetle is a real insect, but it looks like a small worm. It is called a mealworm because it eats "meal", an old name for ground grains and flours, like oatmeal.

Chrysalis hangs off twig

Becoming a butterfly
Butterfly eggs hatch into larvae called caterpillars. Each outgrows its skin and becomes a pupa – known as a chrysalis (*kris-a-lis*) in butterflies. Chrysalises are found hanging from branches or on the undersides of leaves. Many look brown and wrinkled, like old leaves. Inside its case the caterpillar is changing shape. In a few weeks it becomes a butterfly.

The pupa

The larva continues to eat, grow, and moult its skin. After about five moults, it turns into the next stage of its life, a hard-cased pupa. The pupa does not move at all, but inside, the larva is changing enormously.

Antenna

Mouthparts

Claws on feet

Pupa

Inside the pupa, parts of the larva's body break down, then rebuild into a beetle.

Wings are under wing case on back

The adult

After a few weeks, the pupa's case splits open and an adult flour beetle crawls out. Only now does it look like a typical insect, with six legs and wings.

Wings out to dry

When an adult insect like this cicada comes out of the pupa, its wings are all crumpled. The adult pumps blood into them. The wings spread out, and go stiff and hard as they dry. Then the adult can fly away.

Growing up gradually

Some insects don't go through as many stages in growth as others. The young of these insects hatch from their eggs looking like tiny adults. These babies are called nymphs. These nymphs moult their outer skins many times, changing body size slightly at each moult. This is called incomplete metamorphosis. Insects that grow like this include locusts, dragonflies, and bugs.

After the first moult

Hatching
The female locust lays her eggs in a strong case, in the sand. The baby locusts hatch from the eggs and dig their way out.

After the second moult

The nymph's claws hold it firmly on the twig.

Adult's body enlarges as it pulls its long legs out from inside the old nymph legs.

Getting bigger
Every few weeks, the locust nymph moults and then grows before the new skin hardens. It does this four times. It only has small wings and cannot fly. But at the fifth moult, an adult emerges from the skin, complete with full-length wings.

Adult begins to wriggle out of the old skin.

32

Not quite adult

A mayfly nymph lives for years under water, breathing with three tail-like gills. At last it crawls up a plant stem and splits its skin. But it does not become an adult yet. First it moults into a sub-adult, which cannot fly very well. The sub-adult flutters to a bush or tree near the water. In a few hours it sheds a thin skin and becomes the real adult, which can fly much better.

First flight

As soon as its wings have dried, the adult locust can fly away.

The old skin is now almost empty.

Adult hangs onto nymph skin . . .

The nymph skin is perfect in every detail, even down to the antennae and eye coverings.

. . . as it pulls the rest of its body free.

The adult's wings begin to spread out as blood pumps into their veins.

Dangerous insects

Most of the millions of kinds of insects are not harmful. But a few cause problems. Some caterpillars, beetles, and weevils spoil crops and damage trees. Cockroaches infest food stores. Termites weaken wooden furniture and buildings. Some insects kill people by biting and spreading diseases.

Abdomen
full of
blood

Jungle fever
Different kinds of mosquitoes spread the germs that cause malaria and yellow fever. These illnesses affect warm tropical places such as swamps and jungles, where mosquitoes live and breed.

Spreading germs
When a mosquito bites someone and sucks blood, it takes in any germs in the blood. When it bites another person, some of the germs leak into their blood. This spreads the germs that cause diseases.

Beware of the sting
Insects such as bees and wasps have a sharp sting at the rear end. A bee can use its sting only once, but wasps can use their several times.

The hornet, a big wasp, can give a very painful sting – so be careful!

You can recognize the hornet by its yellow and reddish-brown colouring.

The sting pokes out of the rear end as the hornet attacks.

Potato pest

Colorado beetles love to eat potato leaves. If they breed well, they cause enormous damage to potato crops. Originally, these beetles came from the Rocky Mountains in Colorado, United States – which explains their name.

The aphids collect on buds, where the sap is easiest to get to.

The gardener's enemy

Look closer at a flower and you may see this sight – lots of little insects crawling about. These are aphids – also called greenflies and blackflies. Aphids use their spear-like mouths to pierce plants and drink the sap. They breed very fast. When the young hatch, they feed on the leaves and soon the plant shrivels and dies. Aphids feed on roses, beans, cabbages, currants, or other plants.

A newly born aphid, or nymph, is the same shape as its mother.

Quick babies

In early spring, a female aphid does not need to mate or lay eggs. She gives birth to babies, which quickly grow and produce their own young. This is why aphids breed so fast.

Hunting insects

Insects that hunt other creatures need to have large eyes to see their prey, strong limbs to hold it, and powerful jaws to crunch and chew it. Some have stings to poison and paralyze their victims. The hunter on this page is called a praying mantis. It munches on other insects, such as flies – and also other mantises.

How to catch a fly
The mantis keeps perfectly still as it watches a fly. Its green colour makes it look like a harmless green leaf. Even its eyes are green!

Grasping front legs have hooks and spines.

The fly explores the young leaf for food.

The mantis slowly leans forward, holding firmly onto the twig with its two rear pairs of legs.

In a flash, the mantis unfolds and shoots forward its front legs. It grasps the fly in a strong grip.

The fly cannot escape from spikes on the legs.

Assassin bug

The assassin bug hides in a flower. When a victim comes near, the assassin grabs it and jabs its long, tube-like mouth into the body. Poison flows down the tube, dissolving the victim's insides which the assassin sucks up – like you sucking a milkshake up a straw.

Fly feast

The mantis leans back onto its perch and settles down to eat the fly. Its powerful jaws soon cut through the fly's body casing and begin to scoop out the soft flesh from inside.

The mantis's large eyes keep watch for danger, as well as seeing the best way to eat the fly.

Hooks and spines on front legs grip prey.

Strong mouthparts cut up and devour the fly.

The mantis will leave the less nourishing wings and legs.

Parasites

A parasite is an animal (or plant) that lives on or in another, which is known as the host. The parasite harms the host, usually by stealing its blood or other nourishment. Several kinds of insects are parasites. Lice, mosquitoes, and fleas suck blood. Many sorts of wasps are parasites on the eggs, larvae, or adults of other insects.

Weevil hunter
The weevil-hunting wasp chooses big weevils as hosts for its larvae. As the weevil feeds on a flower, the wasp grasps and stings it. The sting paralyzes the weevil so it cannot move – but it does not die.

The wasp holds the weevil in position with its strong legs.

The sting enters where the weevil's body casing is thin, usually at a joint.

A flea can leap more than 30 cms with its strong rear legs.

Leaping bloodsucker

Worm-shaped flea larvae live in dirt and soil. They turn into adults which pierce the skin of their host and suck the blood. Different types of fleas have different hosts. Fleas from cats, dogs, and rats may bite people.

Irritating itch

If a flea bites you, it leaves a red spot on your skin that will itch for a few days. Rat fleas spread diseases such as "Black Death", which once killed millions of people.

The weevil can't move.

Food for the young

The wasp takes several weevils to her nest, in a burrow she has dug in soil. She lays her eggs on the weevils and fills in the burrow. When the larvae hatch, they eat the live hosts.

Weevils in burrow wait to be eaten.

Weevil breakfast

The wasp larvae eat away their hosts' flesh. After a few weeks, the weevils die. The larvae turn into pupae, then into adults which dig their way out.

Living in groups

Have you ever noticed how some insects are never alone? These are called social insects – they need to live in a group in order to survive. Termites are social insects that look and live like ants. They make huge nests, with one queen ruling many workers. Some feed on fungus.

Queen

King

Soldier

Workers are blind and wingless.

Egg machine
The queen termite's body is huge, filled with eggs. She mates with the smaller king, then lays 30,000 eggs each day! She is fed, cleaned, and looked after by workers. Soldier termites with strong biting jaws defend her and the nest.

Mending nests
Many animals, including birds, feed on termites. When they try to break into the nest, workers gather to repair the hole. These termites are mending their nest in a tree-trunk.

A new life
In a big termite colony, some young grow up with eyes and wings. In suitable weather, they fly away to find a mate and start a new nest.

Inside the nest mound

Some termites make their nests underground, or in trees or old logs. Others construct huge mounds with walls of earth mixed with termite spit. The air inside must be cool and moist, or the thin-skinned termites will dry out and die.

The hot air escapes up the main chimney.

Giant tower

The termites' hollow nest-cooling chimney may stand four metres tall. That's much taller than a very tall man!

The walls are made of baked, hardened soil and mud.

A cooling breeze of air flows through the chambers.

Chopped up bits of wood and other food are stored in underground chambers.

Termites feed on fungi (moulds) growing on rotting wood – collected in their own fungus-gardens.

The queen, king, and royal helpers are deep in the nest's centre.

The main nest is below ground level, dark and moist and cool.

Ant society

Scurrying ants are social insects, like termites. The queen ant is the only one that lays eggs. The workers look after her and feed her. They go in search of food – from plants and seeds, to other insects. Big-jawed soldiers defend the underground ant nest.

Tap tap

Ants pass on information about food, enemies, nest damage, and other matters in two ways. They make special chemicals called pheromones (*fer-o-mones*), which other ants smell. And they tap each other with their antennae.

If you see ants touching antennae like this, you'll know that they're "talking".

When at risk, many ants spray a stinging acid chemical from the rear end.

An ant can run very fast because of its long legs.

Cutting leaves

Ants gather bits of food from plants, small creatures, and rotting material. Leaf-cutter ants snip out pieces of leaves, take them to the nest, grow a special fungus on them, and eat the fungus.

Make an ant farm

Borrow ants from nature and watch them for a few days, to see them working together, making a nest and gathering food. Use an empty aquarium tank, old goldfish bowl, or other ant-tight container.

1 Stick dark paper around part of the tank. The ants like their tunnels to be dark, so they are more likely to make them up against the sides in these parts.

2 Look for an ants' nest in the garden, park or meadow. Under a stone is a good place. Gather a few trowel-fuls of ants and soil. Try to get a mixture of different-sized ants.

3 Put the ants and soil in the tank. Add more damp (not wet) soil, a few new and old leaves, and a bit of fruit. Make sure air can get in, but ants can't get out.

4 After a few days, gently lift the dark paper. You may see ant tunnels built up against the glass. Put the ants back where you found them after a week or two.

43

Busy bees

You may have seen honey-bees buzzing from flower to flower. This means that they're collecting food to bring back to their nest or hive (a house built for them by people). Like termites and ants, honey-bees live in groups.

The bee sucks nectar with its tube-shaped mouthparts.

🤚 *Bees can sting — so watch their antics from a safe distance.*

It carries the food back to the hive.

Bee line

When a worker bee finds some flowers that have lots of sweet nectar to collect, it flies back to the hive and "dances" to tell the other workers where it is. Then they fly hundreds of times between flowers and hive.

Bags of pollen

As the bee sips nectar it rubs against pollen grains (yellow powder on flowers). The pollen gets caught on the bee's body. The bee carries the pollen back to the hive in hairy "shopping bags" on its back legs.

Keeping bees

People keep honey-bees so that they can collect their sweet, sticky honey. The bees change the nectar into honey, which they store in honey cells. The bee-keeper removes some combs, and takes the honey.

Inside the hive

A big hive may have more than 50,000 bees. The queen lays all the eggs. Lots of female workers feed and clean her, clean the hive, sting enemies, and look after the eggs and the larvae in their cells. There are also males (called drones). Several drones mate with the queen.

A worker dances by waggling her abdomen, to tell other bees where the nectar is.

Workers make six-sided cells from wax, which comes from glands below their abdomens.

Some cells will contain stored honey, others will hold eggs and growing larvae.

Don't touch!

If you notice a brightly-coloured insect in the park or wood – you are probably meant to! The bright reds, yellows, and oranges, often patterned as spots or stripes, are warning colours. They warn predators such as birds and lizards that the insect has horrible-tasting flesh, that it bites or stings, or that it squirts foul-smelling fluid.

Froghoppers can hop well, like frogs.

Blister bearer

The blister beetle's shiny body warns that this beast tastes bad. If its blood gets on the skin of a person or animal it causes painful blisters. Animals soon learn to leave the beetles alone.

The froghopper's pattern is like the ladybird's, which has black spots on a red body.

Blister beetles gather on flowers to feed and lay eggs.

I taste horrible

Bright red spots on the black body of the red-and-black froghopper mean it tastes horrible. Young frog-hoppers make a ball of frothy "cuckoo spit" to cover them up, as they suck plant juices.

Shields and stinks

Shieldbugs have a hard, shield-shaped covering over the thorax. Some "shields" are green for camouflage, but the orange shieldbug's bright colours make it easy to see as it feeds among the leaves. When in danger, it oozes a stinking liquid.

Shieldbugs are also called stink-bugs – can you guess why?

✋ *The wasp looks like the harmless hoverfly, but has a sting.*

Leave well alone

A young bird or other predator would quickly spit out the nasty tasting orange shieldbug. After a shock like that, it would learn to avoid other orange shieldbugs, and similar-coloured insects.

Pretending to be dangerous

Some insects have warning colours, like this hoverfly, yet they are not harmful. They copy the patterns of harmful insects, such as wasps. Predators who learn to leave wasps alone do the same with hoverflies. This "copying" is known as mimicry.

The hoverfly does not have a sting at its rear end.

Black and yellow

Yellow and black stripes are common warning colours in the animal world. In wasps and bees they advertize their stings. Frogs with them taste awful, and yellow-and-black snakes may be poisonous.

47

A good cover-up

Some insects look like insects. Others don't. They look like bright green leaves, old brown leaves, colourful petals, twigs, buds, thorns, or even birds' droppings. Such a disguise helps the insect to stay unnoticed by predators. Some insects frighten off predators with marks like huge, fierce "eyes".

Prickly problem
Thornbugs suck the sap of plants such as roses and brambles. Their bodies are shaped like the plant's own thorns and prickles, which few predators want to eat!

Thornbugs have to stay still for their disguise to work.

Eyespots look like those on a peacock's tail. This is why it's called the peacock butterfly.

Butterfly or hawk?
With wings folded over its back, in its resting position, the peacock butterfly looks like a piece of bark. But when in danger, it opens its wings and flashes huge eyespots, pretending to be a hawk.

The dark markings on the underside of the wings help it to blend in with the bark.

Thorns are like the insect's spines

Claws on the feet grip the twig securely, even in a strong wind.

The flattened bulges on the legs look like the blades of old, shrunken leaves.

The bent abdomen has spiny edges, like the leaves and twigs around it.

Spiny stick

This giant spiny stick-insect, up to 20 cm long, blends in perfectly with the prickles and curly leaves on which it's perched. So predators ignore it, as long as it stays put on the prickly plant.

Cricket camouflage

The bright colour of the green bush cricket is like the green leaf it sits on. Blending in with the surroundings like this is called camouflage.

Insects in the park

Even the neatest, best-kept park or garden is home to thousands of insects. In the summer you can see them crawling in the soil, climbing up plants, eating leaves, and buzzing or flitting from flower to flower. If it gets cold, they hide in cracks in walls or under roofs.

The beetle defends itself by arching its tail and squirting horrible-smelling liquid from its rear end.

Careful mother

In springtime, earwigs lay their pearly oval-shaped eggs. The mother earwig is one of the few insects that cares for her eggs. She carefully licks them all over, to stop them going mouldy.

Night-time hunter

You won't see the devil's coach-horse beetle by day, unless you look in damp places under stones, leaves, or logs.
It comes out at night to catch tiny caterpillars, worms, and spiders.

The bumblebee sucks nectar up through its tube mouthparts.

Helpful bumble

Insects such as bumblebees visit flowers to collect pollen and nectar. They help the flower by carrying its pollen to other flowers of the same kind, so they can develop into seeds.

The bumblebee brushes pollen onto its back legs, to take back to its nest.

Borrowing insects

To study insects, borrow them from nature using a pitfall trap. You'll need a jamjar, a trowel, and a flat stone. Afterwards, put them back in the same place. Are the same insects active by day as by night?

1 In a sheltered corner, dig a small hole in the ground, just big enough for the jamjar. Put some old leaves in the jar. Find four small stones.

2 Put the jamjar in the hole, its rim at ground level. Place the flat stone over it, propped up on the smaller stones, to keep out rain.

3 During the day, look in the jar every two or three hours. Note which insects have fallen in. Remove the jar when you've finished.

51

Insects in the woodlands

Woodlands are ideal places for insects. The trees provide food and shelter for hundreds of different kinds of insects. Leaves, buds, fruits, and seeds are all food for plant-eating insects. Hunting insects prey on the plant-eaters. Some insects burrow into living wood, or eat moulds growing under loose bark. Others feed deep in roots or rotting wood.

Stag beetle

A stag beetle larva looks like a big, white worm. For three years it lives in an old woodland log or stump, eating the wood. Then it becomes a pupa, and finally an adult. Only males have the huge jaws, which look like deer antlers.

The beetle's huge antler-like jaws are not strong enough to bite you.

The stag beetle has wings under its body casing. You might see one flying on a warm summer night.

Oak-apple galls, made by tiny wasp larvae, look like small green apples that slowly turn brown.

Living in a leaf
Green-oak roller moths are found wherever oak trees grow. The young moths (caterpillars) roll up oak leaves and eat them by the thousands!

Gall wasp – ten times life size

Tree-dwellers
To see tree-dwelling insects more clearly, put a white sheet under a low branch. Knock the base of the branch with a stick (but do not break the branch). Caterpillars, beetles, crickets, and other insects may fall onto the sheet.

Gall-makers
Some tiny wasps, flies, and other insects live, feed, and lay eggs inside leaves, twigs, and buds. The tree grows a tough wall around the eggs, and seals them off. These growths are called galls. They come in many strange shapes. Look out for lumps on twigs and leaves.

Locking horns
The male stag beetle uses its giant jaws to fight off rival males. Sometimes males lock jaws and have a pushing contest. But the jaw muscles are so weak that they cannot harm each other.

The female stag beetle's jaws are small. But she can give a painful bite.

53

Insects in the desert

Deserts are too dry for most animals. But many insects can live there, especially beetles. They usually hide by day, to avoid the hot sun. At night they feed on plants, wind-blown seeds, or each other. Some burrow into desert plants such as cacti. Others feed on the bodies of creatures that died from heat or thirst.

Sandy beetle

This desert darkling beetle is sand-coloured, to hide it from enemies. Its larvae look like worms or maggots, and burrow into the sandy soil, like earthworms do in garden soil.

Sand trap

The ant-lion larva, also called a doodlebug, digs a cone-shaped pit in the desert sand, and hides at the bottom. When an ant tumbles in, the larva grabs it and eats it.

Adult ant-lion

Adult ant-lions look a bit like lacewings. The males of some kinds dance in mid-air in swarms, to attract females at breeding time.

The ant-lion larva squirts special juices into its prey, then sucks out its insides.

Moth and flower

The small yucca moth lays eggs in the flowers of yucca plants, which live in the desert. In doing so, it carries pollen from one yucca plant to another, so the seeds can develop. In return, the yucca moth's caterpillars eat some of the developing seeds.

The beetle's large legs give a good grip on the soft desert sand.

The pollen of the yucca flowers is carried only by the yucca moths.

Long legs for fast scuttling

White wing-covers protect delicate wings beneath.

White on white

The white beetle's colour serves two purposes. It hides it from predators as it scuttles over the white sands. It also reflects the heat of the sun, allowing the beetle to hunt for longer during the day.

Dawn drink

As dawn mist drifts over the desert, the dune beetle runs up a sandhill and tips up its body. The mist forms water droplets on its body – so the beetle gets a drink.

Insects in the water

Next time you're passing a pond or river, take a closer look at the water. For many insects make their homes in water. There are insects that skim over the surface, and ones that swim upside-down. And there are some insects, like dragonflies, that only live in water when they are young.

Keep a lookout – the beetle must come to the surface for air.

Bristles on legs spread out to make "oars" to row the beetle through the water.

The male has a smooth back like this.

The female has grooves on her back.

Clawed front legs for grasping prey

Beetle stores air under wings

Dreaded diver
The great diving beetle lives in ponds and has a fierce reputation. With its powerful jaws, it attacks small fishes and tadpoles, as well as other beetles.

Hard case on back covers two wings

Young dragonfly
The dragonfly nymph lives in the pond for several years after hatching, before turning into an adult. Be careful – it can bite!

Dipping for insects

Dip a net onto the bottom of a pond or river, and sit still. When you see an insect, gently lift your net. Turn it inside out in a bucket with water from the pond or river.

The body and tail bristles trap air for the nymph to breathe.

Approach the water's edge quietly.

Upside-down bug

The water boatman, also called the backswimmer, swims upside down. Look just under the surface to see how it rows along with its bristle-covered legs.

Baby beetle

The diving beetle nymph either walks along the bottom or swims using its legs as oars. It breathes through a long tube in its tail. This works like a snorkel to take in air at the water's surface.

Like its parent (opposite) the nymph is a ferocious hunter.

Caddis case is made of plant stems and mud, glued by sticky silk.

Case for defence

Caddisfly nymphs make cases to protect their soft bodies. While dipping for insects, you may find stones, stems, or shells stuck together. If you look closely you may see a caddisfly nymph inside.

Huge, sharp mouthparts spear tadpoles, small frogs, and fish.

Insects in the tropics

Millions of different kinds of insects live in the jungle. Insects love the warmth and dampness. There are plenty of plants to feed on and hide in and masses of tiny animals to catch. You may often see the largest, strangest, and most colourful insects in these places.

Long legs and claws grip the edges of the leaves.

The rear pair of legs fold back on themselves.

Double disguise

The pink-flower mantis looks just like a beautiful flower and is found on orchids. When small creatures come near to search for pollen or nectar, the mantis grabs them in its fearsome front legs. This special disguise also protects the mantis from creatures that might eat it, such as birds and lizards.

Leaping beetle

The back legs of the frog beetle are long and strong, like a frog's legs. It uses them to leap away from predators. The beetle then opens its wings and flies away to complete its escape.

Eyespot

As big as your hand
Hold out your hand and measure six inches. This is the size of the goliath beetle from tropical Africa. Now hold a medium-sized apple. This is about how much it weighs.

The beetle's clawed legs clasp twigs and leaves as it feeds on tree fruits.

The thorax contains strong muscles for moving big legs and powerful wings.

The goliath beetle is one of the bulkiest flying insects.

A sudden fright
The lantern bug usually has its wings folded. But when danger threatens, it quickly spreads its wings to flash two huge false "eyes". They look like the eyes of an owl. Their sudden appearance frightens off most attackers.

Index

M

NO

P

RS

Cricket

T

W

Colorado beetles

Acknowledgments

**Dorling Kindersley
would like to thank:**
Sharon Grant and Carol
Orbel for design assistance.
Gin von Noorden and Kate
Raworth for editorial
assistance and research.
Jane Parker for the index.

Illustrations by:
Julie Anderson, John Davis,
Nick Hewetson, Mark Iley,
Simon Thomas.

Picture credits
t=top b=bottom c=centre
l=left r=right
Bruce Coleman Ltd: 20t,
26tl; /Jane Burton 12t, 44b,
54tl; /G.Cubitt 40b; /
M.Fogden 42bl, 46tr, 55tr; /
Kim Taylor 40c; /Peter Ward
25tl.
Oxford Scientific Films: /
Kathie Atkinson 19c; /J.A.C.
Cooke 34cl; /Stephen Dalton
14b; /L.S.F. 29c.
Premaphotos: /Preston-
Mafham 18tl, 49bl.